Dedicated to my father who was brutally executed in 1975. May you rest in peace in heaven!

In the beginning was the Word, and the Word was with God, and the Word was God. He was with God in the beginning. Through him all things were made; without him nothing was made that has been made. In him was life, and that life was the light of all mankind. The light shines in the darkness, and the darkness has not overcome it. John 1:1-5 NIV

For God so loved the world that he gave his one and only Son, that whoever believes in him shall not perish but have eternal life. John 3:16

Be perfect, therefore, as your Heavenly Father is perfect. Mathew 5:48

God does not play dice – Albert Einstein

Intentionally left blank

TABLE OF CONTENTS

Introduction

Part I My Life in Cambodia

Chapter 1 Early Years……………….........12
Chapter 2 The Khmer Rouge Reigned of Terror..17

Part II My Life in America

Chapter 3 Arriving in America....................42
Chapter 4 The High School Years...............49
Chapter 5 The College Years......................54
Chapter 6 The Professional Years................57
Chapter 7 The Spiritual Awakening Years...69
Chapter 8 Regression Hypnosis....................95
Chapter 9 Encountered with the Urantia Book..98
Chapter 10 Returning to the Christian Kingdom..100

Introduction

I would like to give a testimony of how I found Jesus in the summer of 1997, June 1997 to be specific. First of all, due to the atrocities or evil acts that I have witnessed from April 1975 to mid 1980 from twelve to seventeen years of age, I have denied all God's existence or any of His manifestations as well as any religions. I became an atheist. Before I move on to how I found Jesus through numbers, I would like to tell you some of the details of the evil acts that I have had to witness or experience.

Both of my parents served in the military. When the communist faction took over Cambodia in 1975, one of the first things that they did was to execute all military officers. My father was one of them. They shipped all the officers to a remote location for mass execution. Fortunately, my father wasn't killed. He came back home with a wounded arm. Three months later, they found him and executed him. This time, it was in my presence. That was the first evil act that I have witnessed. Then they split my family apart. They sent me to work long hours and seven days a week in the rice fields. They didn't provide adequate food. I was almost starved to death.

Due to the war in the country within many factions, including the Vietnamese army, I was pushed into a Thai refugee camp. While in the camp, I joined the orphaned group, and the leader of the orphaned group took me in as his brother. Three months later, my new brother and I landed in the United States, the heaven on earth.

From September 1980 to present, I have been living in the United States. It was very hard at first, but I expected nothing from America. I accepted whatever America offered me, which turned out to be more than I expected. When I first arrived in America, I had nothing. I mean really nothing: no money and no education, and I knew nothing about the English language. One decision that I made that changed the course of my life was to go to school, and I had the determination to stay in school. I spent my first eight years in school while in America. In 1988, I received my degree in Electrical Engineering. My belief in education pulled me out of poverty. Then in the summer of 1997, I found God, or rather God has found me.

In June 1997, on Friday to be specific, the operator of my company in Minnesota called me in to fix the computer software called the State Estimator. I arrived at work around 6 am. I struggled to fix the program for about two hours. This had never happened to me before. Then I heard the "Voice" that said, "Why don't you pray on it!" I said no and I denied the "Voice". Then the "Voice" became clearer and stronger. Out of desperation, I placed my hands on the monitors and said, "Whoever you are, please help me." When I opened my eyes, the program solved and displayed a timestamp, "08:08:08", as a completion time for analyzing the power system or the power grid. I was intrigued with the numbers and thought that these numbers most have a religious meaning involving God. But how do I know which god? Was it Allah,

Jesus, Buddha, or Hindu's gods? I could not confirm it. So, I moved on with other life pressing tasks.

Then, the numbers "888" appeared to me again during lunch time. And then again at around 1pm. That got me thinking, and I entered it in the internet searching engine. The result blew my mind away. It said that "888" is a number that belongs to Jesus as it is a summation through His name of the Greek alphabet. I broke down and cried. I stopped working for the rest of the day and searched and learned about Jesus as well as His Father. Before I went home, I placed my hands on the monitor, said the prayer, gave my life to Jesus, and became the follower of Jesus Christ. Now I am one of the children of God!

Part I: My Life in Cambodia

Chapter 1: The Early Years

My birth was a difficult one. My mother and I almost died during child birth. I was born on September 1962 to working class parents.

Both of my parents were in the Royal police. My father's name was Kuhn. My mother's name was Sareth. They were assigned to a remote town. Life was hard for them when I was born. Therefore, my sisters, brother and I were under my grandparents, my mother's parents, care during the early years of our growing up. My grandparents own a few acres of orange orchard and rice farming land. Life was wonderful for me in the orange orchard. There were a lot of things to play. School was the last thing on my mind. In fact, I did very badly in school. I stayed behind one year in the 1st grade. My grandpa never liked me because I did so poorly in school. I got beat up a lot for doing poorly in school.

I'm not very close to my father's family side. I knew my grandpa on my father side came from Thailand. I believe, he was a

Khmer-Thai. He married to my grandma after the Thai-Cambodia war. I rarely came to visit them, but I visited my grandparents on my mother side all the time. I guess, because they raised me when I was young. I felt really attached to them. And I love them very much.

I'm the oldest child in the family. I have six younger sisters and one younger brother. My sisters' name are as follows: Chantha, Petra (deceased), Ratanak, Kimyear, Khana, Mekmou (deceased) and my brother name is Prany. One of my sisters, Petra, always went along with my parents. She was a pretty one in our family. Chantha was my grandpa's favorite. My grandpa didn't like me much, but he was really cared for my well-being. I was a problem child. I played outside too much and careless about school. I remember, one time I took a long steel wire and rubbed it against a wooden column until it got hot. Then I told my sister, Chantha, that it smelled really good. When my sister smelled it, it burned her skin between her nose and upper lip. My grandpa was really mad at me. He chased me across town, but he couldn't catch me. I didn't come home for a whole day. I was afraid of my grandpa. But my sister would have her revenge on me very soon.

When my grandpa was out of town, my sister, Chantha, asked me to climb and pick a rip fruit from a tree in front of our home. After I dropped her the fruit, she yelled, "Grandpa is back." I slide down from the tree and caught my crotch with a hook along the tree. I was cut badly and it required about ten stitches. My sister and I were very mean to each other, but we still loved each other. We were very close. I remember she shared food with me even when grandpa told her not to do so.

When I was about 5 or 6 years of age, there was a flood in the creek in front of our home. I was playing in the water and got pull into deep water. The pelican that we raised came to rescue me. He swam near me and I held onto him real tight as he swam real hard to the dry land. He saved my life.

In 1970, General Lon Nol took over the country from King Sihanouk while he was on medical leave in France. I heard the coup d'etat on the radio. My friends and I were very sad. We knew that our country would go into civil war. I was worried for my parents. I hoped they didn't have to go into battle. But Cambodia was destined to go into the dark years. It was too late to turn back the clock. Even American government couldn't help much.

When my parents were re-assigned to the city, Battambang, they asked me if I wanted to live with them. I gladly said yes "Pa" and "Mak". Pa stands for father and mak stands for mother in Khmer. It was the first time I got very close to my parents. I believe, the year was 1972. However, I still did very badly in school and was kind of a problem child. I just liked to play outside of the house rather than doing any homework. In fact, I stayed behind one year in the 5th grad because I failed to advance to another level. My parents always said, "If you don't study hard, you'll never get anywhere in life." That phrase really shocked the foundation of my being. I was awakened and began to study very hard. I was trying to catch up with other people my age, especially one of my younger sisters, Chantha. For the next school year, I was ranked third in the class. My parents were so proud of me, and I was so happy. Then the next year my life turned upside down.

Chapter 2: The Khmer Rouge Reigned of Terror

There were a lot people in the city toward the end of the war with the Khmer Rouge. As the Khmer Rouge advanced closer and closer to the city, people tried to escape into the city. The city was swollen with people. There was a shortage of food and housing. People were sleeping along the street.

The Khmer Rouge was bombarding into the city daily. They were usually bombarding into the airport. Every night we ran to the bunker for safety. Every family or house had a bunker nearby. My bunker was in front of the house. It was good for two large families. I was very frighten when darkness came. We knew the Khmer Rouge would bombard into the city. We tried to finish our supper as early as possible.

In April 1975, we tried to celebrate The New Years as normal as possible. The Khmer Rouge seemed to give us a little break during our three days of celebration. They stopped bombarding into the city. I believe, The New Years was on April 12, 13 and 14. We knew the war would be over very soon. We were expecting peace. We were expecting our beloved king to come back into our country and rule again.

Immediately after the New Years celebration, the Khmer Rouge took over the whole country. I believe, it was on April 17. My young life began to turn upside down. I was just twelve years old. I remember overhearing my parents' conversation that our country was at peace at last. Both of my parents served in the military. My father was a captain. His name was Kuhn. I believe, my mother was a staff sergeant. Her name was Sareth. They met during the police academy training for the Royal Police and were converted to Khmer Republic Army personnel after the coup d 'etat by General Lon Nol in 1970.

What my parents did not know was that their lives would have turned upside down in a very short time. The Khmer Rouge marched into the city of Battambang in dirty black pajama uniforms, shoes made of used tires, and AK-47 rifles strapped around their shoulders. They were not very friendly. We did not know how to react except to hang a white flag in front of our home, as suggested by my father, as a means of surrender and a sign of peaceful intentions.

The Khmer Rouge soldiers were so happy and excited about their victory that they fired their rifle into the sky. My grandpa said, "There is going to be trouble tonight." So my family and relative went to seek a safe shelter at the Buddhist temple.

The Khmer Rouge and government soldiers fired their rifle into the sky when the sun went down and darkness covered the city. The night sky was lit up from the tracer bullets. We were excited and afraid at the same. We didn't know what to expect in the morning.

When daylight arrived, the Khmer Rouge immediately ordered male military officers to report to the school south of the city. They said they were going to take them to welcome our king and queen back into the country. I heard from other people that some foot soldiers tried to put on fake officer insignia, so they could join with their high-ranking officers just for this special occasion. They stayed in the school area for a few days. The school was surrounded with many Khmer Rouge soldiers.

My father was suspicious of their intention. I could see it in his eyes. He looked very sad. I tried to cheer him up with delicious foods that my mother cooked for him. Finally, he asked me, "How is your mother doing?" I said, "She's doing just fine, Pa." I told him, "Thing is going to be fine, Pa. You don't have to go to war anymore. No battle for you to fight. Is that great, Pa? We'll be together forever."

My mother and I buried all the military belongings we could find in our home after we heard they would make searches during the first week of the takeover. My parents accumulated a lot of military stuff such as guns, clothing, helmets. They also took a lot of photos in police and military uniform. I remember, I had to dig a big hole under our house to bury all the military stuff. We did all that at night so that the Khmer Rouge soldiers wouldn't spot us. I remember my mother and I were really nervous. We had so many questions like, "If they come in peace, why do they want to make search of our home?" We knew something wasn't right. We began to feel very nervous. We felt uncertain about our future. We heard that they were very cruel to their captive in the past.

I also noticed the Khmer Rouge strange behavior. If they wanted your watch or motorcycle, they just asked for it, and if you don't give it to them, they pointed their gun at you. I heard that some people had lost their life because they refused to give up their belongings. Fortunately, they never asked for our moped.

One day when I brought lunch for my father on my bicycle, the school was emptied. I saw people walking around looking for their husbands and fathers. When I asked them where my father was, they said the Khmer Rouge sent him to welcome our king and queen back into the country. Even though I was young at the time, I suspect something was not right. They kept my father for a few days without a chance to take a bath or change his uniform. I thought, "How can they send someone to welcome the king and queen in dirty uniform?" I used to see people wear white uniforms when they stayed in line to welcome our king and queen, not in a combat uniform.

Soon after they shipped out all the military officers, the Khmer Rough evacuated the city. My mother decided to go back to her hometown, Audambang, which was about ten miles or so from the city. Audambang is a town where my grandparents live and where I used to live with them. My grandparents' home was destroyed by a bomb near the end of the war. I saw my grandparents cry for a long time over the loss of their home. They built a makeshift shelter nearby for the time being. Everything was uncertain. They had very mixed emotions. On top of that, the old government currency had no value, or it took a bag of money to buy anything to cook.

Unfortunately, my mother received news that affected our family of ten forever. I have six younger sisters and one younger brother. My mother called one of my sisters, Chantha, and me to a quiet room and told us that my father was wounded and was being hidden in a remote location in his hometown, Phnom Sompou. I started to cry, and my mother said not to tell anybody, even my younger brother and sisters. My mother decided to be with my father and took care of him. She took my two sisters Chantha and Petra, and me along. The rest of the family stayed with my grandparents.

When I met my father again, about two days later, he looked so frightened and pale. He was a man who was too disciplined to show emotion or weakness, but that was what I saw now. I started to cry again, and my father said, "Don't cry, my son, be strong."

I learned that the Khmer Rough didn't ship my father to welcome the king. Instead, they shipped my father and the rest of the military officers to a remote area northwest of the city near the Thai border. They asked all the officers to stand in formation, and then they mass executed them, without any blindfolds. They used machine guns, rifles, and grenades. Then they shot one by one at anybody who moved.

My father was buried underneath all the dead bodies. Fortunately, only one bullet went through his arm and two bullets stuck in his skull. The bullets that stuck in his skull lost momentum after passing through the other bodies. My father stayed motionless underneath the dead bodies until dark; then he tried to run to his hometown during the night.

My father told me that there was a small bird that led him home. He said this bird would sing and flew from tree to tree. He said he just ran after the bird until he reached his hometown.

The whole family was shocked by this unexpected event. We thought the country was at peace at last, but instead, it was just the beginning of the dark years; years I wished that no one in the civilized world would have had to experience.

During the evacuation period, Khmer society seemed to be in disarray. People tried to find their way out of the city. I tried to load the family belongings onto my bike. I could make only two trips a day between my father's hometown and my home in the city, which were about 25 miles apart, because of the tremendously heavy traffic. Also there was a lot of looting going on in the city. People didn't respect other people's properties, even life itself.

The Khmer Rouge showed no mercy toward any one, young or old, even the very sick ones. They ordered all the sick people out of hospital at gunpoint. They ordered you to get of the car if you had one. They only allowed people to use ox cart to carry their belongings.

One month later people settled down in their chosen town, and everywhere things seemed to be very quiet, except for my family. The Khmer Rouge threatened that if anyone was hiding the enemy, the whole family would be executed. My father's relatives were very nervous. They tried to find a solution for my family. They discussed either poisoning my father, hiding him underground, or giving us an ox cart to try to get to Thailand since my father could speak Thai fluently. The first solution was too inhumane. The second solution was impossible since the rainy season was approaching, and the underground cave would fill with water. The probability of getting caught if they used the third solution was high because traveling was prohibited without a pass.

One event still haunts me even after years of trying to block it out of my subconscious. My father's brother-in-law reached the final solution. He informed the Khmer Rouge soldiers where my father was, and that night twelve soldiers along with my brainwashed uncle, surrounded our cabin. They asked my mother where my father was and she told them he wasn't there. A couple of soldiers climbed up with their flashlights and found him hiding in the corner of our cabin. Immediately they tied my father up and walked him about a thousand feet from our cabin. My mother followed behind them, but they pushed her back and said she should go back and take care of the crying children.

My mother ran to my father's oldest brother, who lived nearby and also had served in the military. When he heard about the incident, he ran to hide himself in the bushes close to where the Khmer Rouge soldiers were with my father. The soldiers then placed my father in the middle of the rice field, pointed flashlights at him, and shot him. My father was still standing after they fired several rounds at him. They walked toward my father and kicked him to the ground and proceeded to bayonet him.

This time, the unforgiving Khmer Rouge did not let my father survive. During the shooting, I heard at least two rounds of fire, which lasted only a few moments, but it seemed like forever. We stayed with our relatives for the rest of the night and waited in fright to verify if he was still alive. Unfortunately, we found his motionless body lying in the middle of the rice field. My father's bullet-ridden and bloodless body lay face up in the 90-degree heat the whole day.

That afternoon we saw a jeep filled with killer Khmer Rouge soldiers passing by my father's motionless and defenseless body. Apparently they had come to verify that my father was still dead. In late afternoon, under the hot and sunny sky, big black clouds suddenly started to form over the town while my father's nephews tried to bury him at the spot where he died. Suddenly, heavy rain and hail began to pour down from the sky. We felt so cold, so afraid, and so fragile without the warm and secure protection of our beloved father.

Life was hard for the first weeks after my father passed away. I lived in fear all the time. We would hide ourselves during the night. We were afraid they were going to kill us too. Some nights we heard the soldier's footsteps, and we would run to hide ourselves. Then we heard gun shot after an hour later. We knew they just executed another person. We ask ourselves, "Are we next?" We cried all the time. We cried so much that no more teardrops came out of our eyes when we cried.

    The Khmer Rouge promoted my uncle to a chief of working group. I guess, they considered him a loyal worker after he informed them where my father was hiding. My uncle assigned me to take care of two cows. I was supposed to feed and bath them daily. He yelled at me all the time when he saw my cows weren't fed properly. He said, "Damn city kid. Doesn't even know how to take care of a cow." He was very mean to us, especially Petra and me. Sometime I saw him beat my sister Petra after she was crying so much for my mother. I remember I thought to myself, "I really want to kill this guy."

About three months later my grandpa reunited us with the rest of the family at my mother's hometown. We passed through the city, which looked like a ghost city except for a few demon Khmer Rouge soldiers riding their bicycles, laughing and smiling at one another. I tried to keep my anger and hatred from showing up. We were even afraid to look at them. We were afraid they might detect what we knew about their unjustifiable actions against their own innocent Khmer people.

During our brief passage through the city, I saw all the modern equipment piling up everywhere: cars, refrigerators, air conditioners, etc. A few months ago, it was a beautiful city. Now, it is the ugliest city that I have ever seen. I saw my school, which was totally empty of any students.

It was getting dark when we got near the edge of the city. My grandpa said, "I'm going to ask those soldiers if we can have some food to eat and a place to stay for the night." I said, "No Grandpa. I'm scared." He said, "It's OK, Grandson. We can't walk in the dark. We'll leave as soon as the sun rise." The soldiers provided food and a place for us to stay. A couple of soldiers kept looking at my mother. I was very nervous. I believe, they knew something about my father. They kept asking my Grandpa, "Where are you from? And where are you going?" I didn't sleep well that night. I tossed and turned all night.

When we heard the roosters cry we all got up. We were anxious to get away from these soldiers. It was too close for comfort. I hated them. I wanted revenge for my father's death. I thought, I was sleeping with my enemy last night. I could have killed some of them while they were sleeping. On the hindsight, I'm glad I didn't act on my urge to kill. They probably would have killed me first. They were professional killers. I had no chance.

For the next three years and eight months my family went through many events that I will never be able to forget. According to the uncivilized and insane Khmer Rouge government, Khmer society was classified as consisting of two types: the old and the new people. The people who they liberated before April 1975 they called the old people, and they provided them with better treatment and living conditions. The people who they liberated after April 1975 they called the new people, whom they treated as their slaves to do all the labor-intensive work without adequate food, supplies, and housing. My family was in the latter group. My mother was forced to remarry, and if she refused, they threatened to terminate her life. Because of my mother's background with the Khmer Republic Army, which they considered to be their number one enemy, she had no choice but to accept the arrangement. My new stepfather and my mother had a son about a year later.

In the meantime, I was sent to a remote farming area with a group of other young boys to build an irrigation system for increasing the rice production. We walked about two days to the work site. We worked from sunrise to sunset, rain or shine. The work was very demanding for a twelve years old boy. The Khmer Rouge played revolutionary song for us. It was an adventure for a young boy like me. At night they gathered us for a meeting and communist indoctrination. I remember, I really hated it. I was tired and hungry. Who could learn in such a condition? They sent me back home after the dry season was over.

When I got back in town, they sent me to grow corn, potatoes and other vegetables at a nearby town. One older boy was very nice to me. They called him a midget. He had a very dark skin. He brought food for me to eat all the time. I thought he liked me. One day, he asked me to sleep next to him. He did not do anything to me for a long time. I felt really secure with this older boy, but then one night he raped me when I was really tired and sleepy. I told my close friend about this incident but he did not seem to care. I also told the Khmer Rouge leader. They just laughed at me. I believe it happened to other young boys as well. This midget did not like me any more after he got what he wanted. At the time, I had no remorse or bad feeling about it. I did not think much about it. I was tired and hungry all the time. I had food on my mind. If somebody killed me, I was probably feeling happy about it. Life had no meaning to me.

In the mean time, one of my sisters was sent to another area with a group of young girls. Two of my sisters died from starvation and disease. My mother had to escape to another safer area called Zone 3, with my new half-brother, since the Khmer Rough was looking for her. We were living in Zone 4, usually referred to as the poorest zone. Sometimes my family would sneak into Zone 3 to ask for food from our relatives. It seemed that the whole country was divided into many zones. Each zone would have its own leadership. Some zones, such as Zone 3, had better treatment and more mercy toward the new people like my family. I heard that other zones were merciless and very cruel toward the new people. They did not provide them adequate food. And on top of that, there were a lot of beatings and killings going on in their zone.

My dispersed family members lived under constant fear and hunger. We were too hungry to show any sign of hatred or revenge. Every night seemed to last forever. It was hard to fall asleep with an empty stomach. Sometimes I filled my stomach with water in order to feel full, so I could sleep easier. As it turned out, I had to get up more frequently to relieve myself. I remember, the other boys and I extended a long tube from our floor to the nearest outside bush to relieve ourselves during the night. Unfortunately, our Khmer Rouge master destroyed our energy-saving device the next morning.

During the day, I would hunt for food like snakes, rats, or anything that moved. This was allowed only during a short break after the long labor-intensive work. My body was so thin and weak from lack of adequate nutrition. The other young boys were in the same condition as mine. We looked like grandpas to one another. We rarely played or had long conversations because we lacked energy, and we tried to conserve it for the next day's work quota.

During the last year under the Khmer Rouge's rule, my sisters, brother, and I joined my mother in Zone 3. While at Zone 3, I was sent to clear new land for growing cotton. There was plenty of food to eat and a lot of tropical fruits to pick. It was the first time that I felt life was worth living, but I was so sad that I never had a chance to see my family at all. It seemed that the whole country was divided into many zones. Each zone had its own leadership but was under one insane and merciless Khmer Rouge government. Some zones, such as Zone 3, had better treatment and more mercy than other zones.

While in Zone 3, I even fell in love with a beautiful young girl. I couldn't remember her name. She was a niece of the commune leader in my workgroup. She would give me food to eat. Sometimes we would sneak into the cotton field together. We hugged, kissed and embraced each other for hours. We were really in love. She was my first love. I really miss her even now. Of all my relationship with women, she was the one I remember the most. I still love her now. I always wonder how she is doing. How many children does she have? If she is still alive, I would like to meet her again.

In late 1978 and early 1979, the Vietnamese army invaded Cambodia, driving the Khmer Rouge government into the jungle in northwestern Cambodia. Without any more Khmer Rouge masters around, my family, immediate relatives, and other people returned to the city to their original homes. Except for cement columns, my home was no longer standing. Our family and some of my immediate relatives stayed in other people's homes.

For those three years and eight months of living under the inhumane treatment of an insane Khmer Rouge government, every day seemed like months, months seemed like years, and years seemed like centuries. Time seemed to be at a standstill. There was no schooling and no prospect for the future. The only things I learned were hatred and revenge for my father's and sisters' deaths. Even after 35 years, I'm not so sure I can say the word *forgive*, but I surely will never forget what the

Khmer Rouge did to my family and their own Khmer people. I hope such an insane government will never rule Cambodia or any civilized country again.

In 1979 life was hard for our family. The hunt for food was the major concern in our daily life. The question in everyone's mind was, "Where are we going find food and feed ourselves?" I was the oldest child so I became a father figure to my younger siblings. I had to find a way to feed them. It was a major responsibility for a 17 years old boy who just came out of hell that the Khmer Rouge had created. I didn't have any useful skills. All I had was the energy from my skinny body. I said to God," "Why God? Why did you let them take my father away from me?" I was so jealous of the other families who still have their father with them. It was about this time that I begin to have a strong negative feeling toward God. I hated Him. I cursed at Him. And I didn't think He existed. I thought to myself, "If God exists, He would not let such evil exist on earth."

Part II: My Life in America

Intentionally left blank

In transition camp to America

Chapter 3: Arriving in America

In 1979, my family settled at my grandparents' home. The Khmer Rouge built several homes on our property. I'm very thankful that there were homes on our old property since I just turned 17 years old and lacked the skill to build a home on my own.

Since I'm the oldest child in the family, I became a father figure to the rest of my siblings. I had to feed them plus my mother and grandma. There were not many jobs that I could perform. I forgot how to read and write. Fortunately, a family that stayed on our property taught me how to climb palm trees and collect sweetens juice from them to refine into brown sugar. I had ten palm trees to collect the juice from. Everyday my mother would take our sugar to the market and trade for any necessities. We depended on the palm trees for our living for about a year.

Then an unexpected event struck our family again. My brown sugar could not compete with the high quality white sugar imported from Thailand. My sugar dropped in price drastically. I guess that was the first time I experienced a market economy. In addition, the Vietnamese army wanted to kill me for letting a prisoner escape. I joined the militia and one night we captured a freedom fighter. I was assigned to guard him from 1am to 3am and I fell asleep. The next morning, the Vietnamese army was looking me. My friend told me to escape.

    I asked my mother if my stepfather could move in with her so that I could venture into the outside world at the Thai-Cambodian border as well as escape from the Vietnamese army. My mother was afraid to ask my stepfather to come back with her. I told her I would be willing to do that for our family. She said "Yes, my son."

    When I asked my stepfather to come to live with my mother, he said, "Yes, my stepson. I'll be happy to be with your mother again." My stepfather and my mother were separated when my mother escaped to Zone 3 during the Khmer Rouge reign of terror. My mother, my stepfather and I made a long journey to the new world, that is what I called it then, together. Fortunately, my mother knew a close friend of my deceased father at the camp. He was in charge of all the police force in the border camp called Nang Chan. I became the policeman in charge of distributing rice and other goods to the needy.

About three months later, the Vietnamese army destroyed my camp at Nang Chan. I ran into Thailand and proceeded to sneak into the Khou-I-Dang camp in Thailand. The camp didn't allow any more refugees. There were Thai military guards at the camp. They shot at anybody who tried to get into the camp. I was very afraid when I tried to sneak into the camp. When I got inside the camp, my relatives were waiting for me. It was a very joyful time to be re-united with my relatives.

My aunt had an adopted son, Siphan, who was in charge of the orphans in the camp. His name was on list to go to America within a few weeks. My aunt said, "Siphan, why don't you take Vuth along?" He said, "Why not?"

But I had to be a minor. I was almost 18 years old, so my foster brother gave me a new name and date of birth.

About three months later, I arrived in America, my new "new world", with my foster brother. I thought my new world would end at the Thai-Cambodian border. Instead, it ended on the American soil.

When I look back at my life, I seemed to notice that there were a lot of coincidences and synchronicities. It seemed that someone helped me along the way. I thought the help came from my father for a long time. That assumption was confirmed when I did a regression hypnosis on March 17, 2006. My father was always with me as my spiritual guide.

My first arrival on American soil was in Seattle, Washington. I couldn't believe my eyes when I first arrived there. There were beautiful white people, tall buildings and a lot of cars. I thought, "Oh, I'm really in heaven." I had already stopped believing in God since they killed my father. But when I saw Seattle, my first thought was "This is heaven." After what I went through during the Khmer Rouge years, you can't blame me for not believing in God anymore.

Then we flew to Los Angeles, California, in order to meet with our sponsor, but when we arrived there, she didn't show up. Someone else came to welcome us. We stayed in the hotel for a couple weeks until they located another sponsor for us. Finally, we got word that we're moving to Rochester, Minnesota.

We flew to Minnesota after a couple days of waiting for paper work to be worked out. When the airplane almost reached the runway for a touchdown, I saw endless acres of cornfield. I thought to myself, "Ha, I'm going to work in the cornfield, picking up those corns. This is great." I learned later on that they already had a combine to harvest them. They didn't need the energy from my skinny body. They had machines to do the hard work.

While at the Rochester's airport, my sponsor, Mary, and one Cambodian fellow welcomed us to America. My sponsor, Mary, told me through a Cambodian translator, to call her "mom." She is beautiful, and I love her as my own mom. She took us to our first apartment and then took us to do some grocery shopping. I've never been in American grocery store before. There were a lot of foods. I was so happy, but I was a little sad that my real mom wasn't here with me.

For the first couple of years we depended on the public assistance and food stamps. I cooked food for both of us. I gained weight rapidly. My skin tone changed color, too, from dark to light.

In 1981 my aunt, uncle and one of my sisters, Ratanak, joined us in Rochester, Minnesota. It was a very happy time. There was a lot of food for everyone. I said, "Now we don't have to worry about not having enough food to eat." We just hugged each other all day long. We always thank the American people for being so generous to us.

In 1982 my grandma, sister and brother joined us again in Rochester, Minnesota. It was another very happy time. Again there was a lot food being served to everyone.

Between 1982 and 1983, I had a newspaper route. I made enough money to buy my own necessities. I always looked up to Christmas season when my customers gave me tips for doing a good job. I tried to deliver the newspaper rain, shine or snow.

Within a few weeks of my arriving in America, I was sent to high school.

Chapter 4: The High School Years

In September 1980, I attended high school without even knowing all the English alphabets. I couldn't even count up to ten, so I was put in a special class called English as Second Language (ESL) with the rest of the other refugees. I was in a 10th grade level. The first year was very hard. I felt like I was just born again. I had to learn everything.

I was determined to succeed and finish high school as the rest of the American kids. My father's voice was still echoing in my mind then, "If you don't study hard, you'll never get anywhere in life," and his final words, "Don't cry, my son, but to be strong." Those words motivated me to succeed on my long term goal which was to be self-sufficient and prosper in life.

I studied day and night, even on the weekend. Each day I picked ten or more words from the Khmer-English dictionary and studied them. I memorized the definition and wrote them out ten times each. What I was really doing was forcing as much words as possible into my brain. Then I started reading children's books. After that I proceeded to read the adult books. My method was kind of cruel and tedious, but it seemed to work for me. I was able to build up the vocabulary tremendously, but I lacked the oral communication skill. People had a hard time understanding my English. I was very frustrated. Then I turned to TV, especially Sesame Street program on PBS.

During my 11th grade in high school, I began to venture into the mainstream classes. I always carried Khmer-English dictionary with me. I remembered some American kids really made fun of me, but I just ignored them. Sometimes they called me names like "Geek," and "Rice eater." I tried to ignore them. Sometimes I wished they knew a little bit of what I had been through, so they would not try to hurt my feelings but instead become my friend.

However, I did have some friends. It was my opportunity to practice my English speaking skill. They were very nice to me. One time, they asked me to church with them. I said, "What is a church?" They told me, "Church is where we are going to learn about Jesus or God." Then they added, "Jesus can save your life and soul." I asked, "Who is Jesus?" They told me, "Jesus is the Son God, and we would like for you to come with us this Sunday." I thought to myself, "God? I hate God. He let the Khmer Rouge kill my father. I don't think he existed. Do I want to go with my new friends?" Well, I decided to go with them so that I could practice my English. I wasn't into this Jesus idea.

My new friends picked me up at about 9:30 am on Sunday. We drove to their church for the 10:00 am services. They introduced me to their family and friends. I was very nervous. My English was bad. I didn't think they would understand me much. Then the 10:00 o'clock services arrived. We went inside and seated ourselves. They played some music, then it was time to read the bible. I couldn't read it. It was like it was in another language. It was the King James Version. I went with them for a few more times, then I quit going again. I just couldn't take it any more. The idea of God and Jesus as a Son of God who would save my life and soul was kind of ridiculous. First, I needed proof that God existed.

During my 12th grade year, I took all mainstream classes such as American History, Physics, Algebra, English Composition, etc. It was the first time I felt high school was fun. I learnt to relax a little bit. I watched TV a little bit more. I went to the movie sometimes and I even found time to work a part-time job at my high school as an Audio Visual Assistance. I also still had newspaper route, and I mowed the lawn for my neighbor for a fee. I remember one time my customer left me a note to pull the weeds around the trees after I mowed the lawn. I didn't understand the note, so I pulled all the flowers around the trees. I felt really bad after I found out what they really wanted.

In 1983 I graduated from high school with a C average. My counselor told me that I should become an electronic technician. He thought I would be really good. I told him I wanted to be an engineer. He just shook his head. He said I don't have a strong background in mathematics, physics and science. I was determined to be an electrical engineer at all cost. I was willing to sacrifice anything. I applied to two community colleges, one in Rochester, Minnesota and the other in Elgin, Illinois. Both colleges accepted me into their pre-engineering program. I chose to go to Illinois because my friend, who is an engineer, is there. I was hoping he would help me with some of my homework.

Chapter 5: The College Years

My first one and half years in college was fun. I did OK. I got some A, B and C grades in my college courses. I was a B average student. My GPA would be higher, if I didn't get F for my English class. In fact, I got three F's in my English classes.

However, I missed my family in Minnesota. Therefore, I decided to transfer to the University of Minnesota (U of M). Unfortunately, I couldn't get into the college of engineering at the University of Minnesota due to my low GPA. I decided to attend the liberal art college and try to improve my GPA. The class at the U of M was big, and the students were not that friendly. I didn't have any friends there. Thus I decided to transfer to Minnesota State University (MSU) in Mankato, Minnesota.

I was glad I transferred to MSU. Everything was just right for me: small student body, small class side, friendly professors and student, etc. I also had a part-time job working at the library. The income from that job helped to pay for the food and clothing while I was in school. I was very poor compared to other student. But I was very rich compared to people back home in Cambodia. So I never really complained about anything. I rarely told anybody what I went through back in Cambodia. I had a lot of friends and we formed a study group. I considered my time in college a fun experience. I really enjoyed it. I absorbed knowledge like a sponge absorbed water. I remember I would eat a lot of good foods such as meat during the final exam week. I found eating a lot of meat helped my mind to concentrate better.

In 1986 I met a blonde woman named Kerry in a psychology 101 class. I had this loving feeling for her. I gave her a ride home after class at least once a week. We talked quite a bit, but I never told her about what I went through in Cambodia. I learned that she just broke up with her boyfriend. I said, "I'm so sorry to hear that." She said, "It's alright. He's such a jerk anyway." I wanted to ask her to go to the movie, but I was afraid of the rejection. I thought, "I'm not good enough for her. She is so beautiful. I'm a poor and ugly guy. What am I thinking?" I never met her again after the class was over. I knew where she was living, but I was afraid to stop by to see her again.

It seemed that God likes to send me a blonde woman my way. As you continue to read this book, you'll notice that God also sent me another blond woman to awaken my soul. Even my regression hypnosis therapist is also a beautiful blond woman.

In June 1988, I graduated from MSU. I was so happy. I thought to myself, "Yes, I made it."

Chapter 6: The Professional Years

After my graduation from college in 1988, I obtained a job as an electrical engineer with the electric and gas company in Minnesota. I remember, I sold my old car for $400 to buy a suit for the job interview. I got a job offer from my first interview. I remembered, I accepted the offered right away. I couldn't wait to have that big paycheck. I bought a brand new Toyota, too. Life was wonderful, but it was short lived.

My colleagues couldn't understand me due to my strong accent. One day my boss asked me to go to lunch with him. I couldn't finish my lunch when he said, "Savuth, if you don't improve your English communication skill, we will have to let you go." I was shocked, but I wouldn't let that bother me. I've been through harder times than that. Then my boss added, "You can attend any classes that you like, and we'll pay for them." That was very nice of him to offer me that option. I took a one-on-one lesson with a speech communicator for about two years. It really helped me, but what really help me the most was talking to my colleagues during day-to-day interactions. Life was wonderful again. I had gotten promoted a couple of times during the first five years with the company.

In 1994 I saw an article in the Asian-American press, which stated, "Dith Pran would like any adults who were children during the Khmer Rouge reign of terror to submit their story to be compile into a book." Dith Pran life story during the Khmer Rouge was depicted in the movie called, "The Killing Fields".

I was so excited. I called Dith Pran right away. I explained to him what had happened to my father and family. He said, "Write your story and submit to me as soon as possible." I asked him if anybody had submitted their story. He said, "No." I said, "I would like to be the first to submit it." I didn't make it. It was very hard for me to write about my experiences during the Khmer Rouge reign of terror. I cried a lot, but finally, I was able to write about five pages of my experiences during the Khmer

Rouge reign of terror. I submitted to Dith Pran and made it to number seven on the list. I wanted to be number one on the list, so people would read my story first. The book is called, "Children of Cambodia's Killing Fields: Memoirs by Survivors"

Many things happened in 1994. My mother came to visit us from Cambodia. The re-union was broadcasted on many local channels in the twin cities, Minnesota. It was a very happy time for our family and relatives. Again, food was everywhere. My mother said, "Why is there so much food? Don't waste it." I said, "Mother, please eat as much as you like. There is plenty more to come." My mother gave me a big smile and a hug.

In 1989, I married Melissa. She also came from Cambodia and a survivor of Khmer Rouge reign of terror. We have three children together; two daughters, Valerie and Veronica and a son, Richard. I love all of them, but just like any parents, we all have our favorite one. My son is my favorite one.

Since our marriage, Melissa and I have been separated a couple of times. In 1995, we were separated for the first time. She filed a restraining order against me. I hit my wife after a heated argument. She wanted my mother to move out of the house, she didn't get along with my mother. I said, "No, she is my mother. She is staying with me."

She called 911 after I hit her. My children were crying. Then the police came to our house. They separated my wife and me to a different area. Then they talked to my wife for a while. After they talked to my wife, they came to ask me, "Did you hit your wife?" I said, "Yes" Then they read my rights and handcuffed me. My mother was crying and said, "My son, my son. Don't go." I told her, "Mother, I'll be OK. Don't worry."

As the policeman took me to jail, I cried and cried. I asked myself, "Why? Why do I have to go through many pains and suffering? When will it end? How am I going to end it? It seemed that I came into this world crying and I continued to cry for most of my waking life.

I was afraid when they booked me in jail. I was afraid I would get raped again by someone. The policeman sensed my nervousness and he tried to calm me down. He said, "Things are going to be OK. This is a light security prison."

I was crying all night as I laid there on the hard and cold surface in the prison cell. I couldn't go to sleep. Many things came to my mind. I thought, "What did I do wrong in the previous life that is causing such a pain and suffering in this life time? Is God trying to punish me for cursing at Him?" I thought, "God, you're not doing any good by punishing me some more. I hate you. I hate you. Leave me alone."

When I got out of the jail, I took my mother to California. We went to visit her sister and relative. My mother looked so sad. Sometimes I saw a teardrop from her eyes. Then she said, "Son, I want to go back home." I said, "Mother, you can't go back. Our family is here now. We'll be happy together again.

Things will be fine. I promise. This is your home." She said, "No, son. I can't stay here. I miss my home. Please let me go." I said, "Alright, Mother, I can't keep you here. I can't make you happy here. I'll get you a ticket for Cambodia tomorrow."

It was sad to see my mother departing back to Cambodia. I thought, "I'm going to miss her a lot. I don't know when I am going to see her again." We hugged and cried for a long time.

My mother went back home by herself. I was afraid she was going to get lost, so I looked around at the airport for any Cambodian who was going to Cambodia. I found an older gentleman. I asked him if he would take care of my mother until she got to Cambodia. I told him she didn't speak any English. He said, "Don't worry I'll take care of your mother." I said, "Thanks."

When I came back from California, my wife decided to move to Massachusetts with her mother and sisters. Life was hard for all of us. My daughter Veronica kept calling me all the time and said, "Daddy, I want to go home." She made me cry, and my heart harden.

In February 1996, I filed for bankruptcy when many creditors called me day and night. I couldn't pay all the monthly bills plus a child support payment. My self-esteem was at the lowest point since I arrived in America in 1980. I went to college so that I would have a good paying job. I wanted a life of self-sufficiency. I wanted the American dream, but everything seemed to work against me. I asked, "Why? Why? What did I do wrong? Do I need help from God in order to have happiness?" Then it just dawned onto me, "I have nobody to turn to any more except God." I remember my high school friends were trying to bring me to Christ, but now I began to wonder who Jesus was. I said to myself, "I'll learn about His life soon."

After about a year, I asked my wife to come back home and try to work things out. She agreed. I flew to get them right away. We were very happy to be together again, but it was short lived.

The relationship between my wife and me began to go sour again. We seemed to disagree on many things, even on religion. She has a strong belief in Buddhism, but she doesn't believe in God as all Buddhist do. I hated God, and she doesn't believe in God, and that's what we had in common. My wife always said, "We shouldn't have married. The fortuneteller was right." According to the Chinese zodiac, we were not compatible to be husband and wife. I was born in the tiger year. She was born in the monkey year. Also the fortuneteller said, "If you decide to get marry, you will be separated, even dead." I didn't believe all that nonsense. I thought to myself, "I'm a man of science, this is a bunch of crap." I told Melissa, "I don't believe it. We love each other. That is what is important."

I moved to the basement during this rocky time period. It was hard to sleep in the basement. It smelled. It was cold. I remembered, I cried a lot. I asked myself,

"Why? Why? Why can't I find happiness in my life? I went to college and have a good job, but I still have many problems."

In February 1997, I went to a leather store, Wilson Leather. There was this young beautiful blond woman who came to greet me. She was very nice to me. She asked me, "How can I help you?" I said, "Oh, I'm just browsing around." I walked around the store, and she was following me. I stopped and started to chat with her. We had the eye-to-eye contact for the first time. There was something in her eyes that seemed to steer my soul. I said, "You remind me of someone." She just smiled at me. Then I said, "Yes, you remind me of my sister." I thought to myself, "Those are Petra's eyes." I had mix emotion about this woman. I wanted her to be my sister. On the other hand, I felt some sexual love towards her. Her name is Melissa, like my wife's name. I remember I came to see her everyday. One time, I gave her $100. She refused to accept it, but I said, "Please take it. Would you be my sister?" She finally accepted. We became close, and she invited me to her apartment one night. We just talked and talked for a long time. I learned that she came from Hebing, Minnesota. We were planning to start a business together; although our relationship was meant to end.

In March 1997 I had an episode where I rammed another vehicle and was chased the state troopers on the freeway. I couldn't go to sleep for a long time. This blond woman, Melissa, was on my mind all the time. Then on March 15, 1997, I began to hear a lot of voices. I couldn't sleep, so I got up at about 4:00am and took a shower. Then I went to Amber's restaurant for breakfast. I ordered pancake, eggs and sausage for Melissa, the blond woman. When I knocked at her door, a black man answered the door. I said, "I just like to give this to Melissa." He said, "Leave it at the door." So I left the breakfast at the door and left. I cried and asked myself, "Why? Why? Melissa Why?" That same day, everywhere I went I heard voices that told me to do this and that. The whole episode will be detailed in the next chapter.

In May 2004 my wife and I separated again. This time I moved to a trailer home in Landfall, Minnesota. Both of us were happy. Even my children noticed a change in our relationship. We seemed to care for each other well-being. We didn't file for a divorce. There was no reason to do so. We had no intention of getting involved in another relationship. We're trying to stay together for the children's sake.

When I look back at my life, it had a lot of ups and downs, more downs than ups though. But I guess, that is what life is all about. If there is no pain and suffering, there is no happiness. That is the quality of our existence: happy and sad, love and fear, beauty and ugliness, positive and negative, etc. I'm trying to live my life at the positive end of the polarity such as love, beauty, compassion, kindness, etc. It was hard to live that life without some kind of help. I was so arrogant about myself. I thought, I need no help from anybody, even God. I was wrong. I found out that my relationship with God really helped me to be a better husband, father and person.

Through love, we will be creating heaven on earth. This is what God meant for us to live our life on this earth.

I believe, my episode in March 1997 was a spiritual awakening for me. I rediscovered God. I was seeking God's favor. I prayed. I went to churches searching for God and happiness. In all, I fell in love with God. I used to hate Him so much that it would boil my blood if anybody mentioned the word "God" to me. I believe, Melissa, the blond woman working in the leather store, was an angel. God must be sending her to awaken my soul.

Chapter 7: The Spiritual Awakening Years

Now I would like to give a testimony of my encounter with God or Jesus Christ. I'm an engineer and very good with numbers. God knows that, and he sent his Son Jesus to awaken me to the spiritual way of life and to believe in him through the triple number '888'. As you may already know, I stopped believing in God during the Khmer Rouge's reign of terror. But now, I love and believe in Him.

It all began in 1988, but I didn't realize it until 1997. Here is how God gave me the signs of his presence or existence. The triple number '888' kept appearing to me until I realized that it belonged to Jesus. Each letter of Jesus' name written in Greek has a value which adds up to '888'. For example, I started working for my first employer on 8/15/88 and the start date on my monthly time sheet is printed out as "08-88". I always wondered about that triple number every month.

However, my radical spiritual awakening happened in March 1997. I could not go to sleep for seven nights and on March 15, 1997, I began to hear a lot of voices in my head. For example, while I was driving my van, the voice told me to turn on the radio, which I did. The station that came on the air was a Christian station, and the speaker appealed to the public to open their hearts to the Lord Jesus Christ. That really caught my attention, but I didn't pursue it much further.

My second encounter with the triple number "888" was more interesting. In June 1997, the operator of my company in Minnesota called me in to fix the computer software called the State Estimator. I was unsuccessfully trying to fix this software. I tried everything I knew but to no avail. Then a Voice in my head told me to pray on it. I said no and I denied the Voice. Then the Voice became clearer and stronger. Out of desperation, I placed both of my hands on the monitors, closed my eyes and I said, "Whoever you are, please help me". To my surprise, when I opened my eyes, the computer program, which cycles every eight (8) minutes and keeps the time of the last successful run, worked again. The time stamp on it was 8 hours, 8 minutes and 8 seconds, "08:08:08", hence, the triple number "888". I was intrigued with the numbers and thought it was involved with God. But how do I know which god? Was it Allah, Jesus, Buddha or Hindu's gods? I could not confirm it. So, I moved on with other pressing tasks.

My last encounter with the triple number "888" was at the Asian grocery store. I wanted to return a can of soda back into the cooler, but I dropped and damaged it, so I had to pay for it. When I got the change back, the total was 8 dollars and 88 cents; Again, the triple number "888". By this time, I thought, "This can't be just a coincidence". After I got back to my office, I went on the internet and typed "888" in the Yahoo search engine. That was when I discovered that the triple number "888" is a number that belongs to Jesus: whereas, the number "666" belongs to the Beast as written in the Bible. I was shocked. I became a Christian after I went on the internet and read about the life of Jesus. I remember I cried a lot while I read the story of His life. I realized that Jesus had been through a lot in life. The information on the internet said, "Jesus is a Son of God." I thought to myself, "How can I learn more about the life of Jesus?" Thus I began to attend the church.

In addition, in 1997 I had an episode with the law and with the dark energy (as my hypnosis therapist told me) where I rammed another vehicle on the freeway. It all got started on February 1997 when I met a blond woman. Something in her eyes steered my soul. She reminded me of my deceased sister, Petra. I became restless and having sleeping problems. Then I went through seven nights without sleeping. On March 15, 1997, I began to hear a lot of voices as I described some of them above. Below is an excerpt from the local newspaper, Pioneer Press:

"Usually, the cop chases the bad guy. Smokey and the Bandit, in that order. Last month, in a strange twist, it happened the other way around when a suspect allegedly tried to ram a State

Patrol car from behind. A frightening chase then ensued, exceeding 100 mph at some points before coming to an end in Shoreview.

The backward police chase began on Interstate 694 at about 10:40 pm on March 15. Benjamin Cook was driving home on I-694 near Minnesota I-120 in the northern St. Paul suburbs in his pickup truck – towing a brand new snowmobile on a trailer – when the driver of a Nissan minivan began ramming into him, authorities said. Cook called 911 on his cellular phone, and State Trooper Christopher Edstrom and Lt. Ken Urquhart soon arrived to help.

The troopers watched as the driver of the van – later identified as Savuth Penn, 32, of Oakdale – continued to ram Cook's truck near I-694 and U.S. 61. The troopers then tried to stop Penn, beckoning to him and signaling with their sirens and lights. Penn initially slowed down and appeared to be stopping for the officers. Urquhart then pulled to the side of the highway. But that wasn't the end of the encounter.

"I looked in the (rearview) mirror, and he was coming right at me." Urquhart said in an interview Wednesday. Urquhart accelerated to more than 100 mph, worrying that he would get rammed because his new squad car was not picking up speed quickly enough. At one point, he suddenly lurched his squad car to the left, avoiding a collision.

Penn then continued the chase on the freeway. "He tried to get me I don't know how many times," Urquhart said. The chase continued up the interstate's Lexington exit ramp in Shoreview, where the trooper was forced to run a stoplight to elude Penn, authorities said. Penn kept up the pace, however, whipping through the intersection at 80 mph and down the freeway entrance ramp.

At that point, Penn lost control of his van as it spun out and rolled over. The troopers found Penn, who was not wearing a seat belt, sitting on the passenger side window in his overturned vehicle. He was digging through some bags, looking for something. He began screaming and trying to kick out the windshield as the troopers ordered him to remain still. After a struggle, Penn was arrested.

Urquhart had a burning question for Penn when he and Edstrom arrested him. "What were you doing?" he asked in dismay. Penn looked right through him, Urquhart recalled, and said "God sent me on a mission."

After the incident, Penn, who suffered no physical injuries in the crash, underwent a mental health evaluation, according to authorities."

I was passed out in the ambulance. On the way to the hospital, I heard a voice calling me to wake up. The voice said "Wake up Adam, wake up!". When I woke up, all I remembered were the words "Wake up Adam!". Adam became my nickname ever since.

After I was diagnosed as having a mental illness called bipolar and released from the hospital, I read about that unfortunate incident in the newspaper and what strikes me the most was the phrase "God sent me on a mission." I just couldn't remember saying that to the police officer. That led me to see a regression hypnosis therapy on March 15,

2006, my 9th anniversary of that unfortunate episode. The results of regression hypnosis really shock the foundation of my being. More details of my hypnosis session have been written in chapter 8.

I always denied the doctor's diagnosed. I believed, I had a spiritual awakening. The doctor didn't think so. They said I had a psychosis (maniac) episode, and I was hallucinating things. I said to myself, "Hallucination? Are you kidding me?" It was real to me. I thought to myself, "What is reality?" What we see is just a reflection from light that bounced off the matter. Our mind perceived that as reality. I believe, my mind perceived more than just light bouncing off the matter. I heard voices from another realm, spiritual realm where God resides. In another words, I may have heard the voice of God.

On January 2001 I went to Cambodia for a visit. It was quite an experience to come back home with thousands of dollars in my pocket. I wasn't that poor boy when I left in 1979 anymore. Everything was cheap. People treated me like a king, especially women. They worshipped me like an Angel that just came down from heaven. I really loved the attention. I never had this feeling before. I gave money to the poor like there wouldn't be tomorrow. I went to see my mother at her hometown for a few days. I also went to see my father's relatives at his hometown. Before I left for America, I went to see the Angkorwat, the famous temple in Cambodia. Eight months later 9/11 struck in the heart of America.

September 11, 2001, tragedy shocked the foundation of my being again. I asked God, "Why, God, why?" Since I believe things happened for a reason. In other words, there is a purpose for things to happen. It is either good or evil.

After 9/11 tragedy, I started to notice the number "11" or "11:11". After my experience with the triple number "888", I gave great attention to such occurrence. I believe, there must be a message from somewhere, another realm, or the universe, or even from God Himself.

Since 1997 I was totally changed. I heard a lot of voices. My therapist said it was due to my mental illness; but I always denied what he said. I believed the voices came from the other realm, good and bad. I just needed to tune into the friendly voices. I need to learn to filter out the bad or evil voices such as the voice that told me to ram the other vehicle on March 1997.

During 1997 to 2004, I went to many different churches such as the Assembly of God, The Cambodian Nazarene Church, Catholic Church, Mormon church, etc. I was baptized four times. I did not feel satisfied with the organized churches. I still felt the emptiness in me. In fact, they created fear in me. I feared that I may not go to heaven.

My pastor said the bible was the words from God and everything was true. But I had a burning question of what Jesus said, "**I'm the true, the way and the life, no one goes to the Father except through me**." That meant that nobody goes to heaven without believing in

Jesus. I thought to myself, "What happens to Buddhist, Muslim and other people who have a different belief system? Do they go to hell? This is not right." I thought the bible must contain some distortion. I asked other Christians about that issue. They told me, "They go to hell if they didn't follow Christ when they died." Then I asked them about my father. I briefly told them about my father. They told me, "I'm sorry; he went to hell because he didn't know Christ when he died." I was so disturbed.

I tried very hard to convert my family to believe in Jesus. I did not succeed. My wife is a strong believer in Buddhism. I gave up. Also my search for God at all churches came to an end. Finally, after many years of searching for God at many churches, I didn't find Him there. I found Him in my heart. He is always with me. I was just looking for Him at the wrong places. After I knew that He is in my heart, I was trying to make the longest journey to reach Him. That longest journey was between my head down to my heart. It was a very hard journey. It took me a long time. I finally succeeded through a simple act of LOVE and FORGIVENESS. I forgave all the people who had hurt my family and me since 1975. I felt at peace with myself. I said, "May your soul find peace in heaven. God bless you all."

There is a plan to bring the Khmer Rouge to trial for genocide against humanity. I used to support that idea back in 1995. I sent many letters to the Senators, asking them for their supports. I got many responses and supports.

Now, I believe we should just ***forgive*** them and send them the energy of LOVE. I believe they didn't know what they were doing. They let hatred take control of their conscience and soul. I remember when I was working as an engineer in 1995, I thought to myself, "If I have the possession of the atomic bomb, I would not be hesitant to use it at their strong hold in Cambodia. I can use the satellite technology to pinpoint the where about of Pol Pot and drop the bomb there." I even learned how to fly an airplane just in case I needed one. In actuality, I let my hatred take control of my conscience and soul just like them. When I look back to 1995, I was glad I didn't act on my hatred toward the Khmer Rouge.

In my regression, I met my earthly father and other light beings. I saw my father as a golden being. I knew then that he is in heaven with God. He is not in hell as my Christian friends had told me.

Then my Christian life was about to change. I was a Christian since 1997. I went to the church almost every Sunday. I tried to read the bible everyday. I loved to read about the bible prophecy. I even thought about becoming a bible prophecy scholar.

One night, I had a dream of a golden being coming to embrace me. He/she, I couldn't identify its sex, put his/her right arm over my shoulder. He glowed as bright as a sun. He has no hair. I was frightened, and I yelled so loud that my whole family woke up. I thought he was a ghost. I found out from my regression hypnosis that he was my deceased father. He is also my spirit guide as stated in my regression session.

This dream really disturbed me, so that I went to the elders at the temple to consult them for its meaning. The elders said, "It means that the Buddha wants you to come back home to our religion. Our religion is your home." My life took another turn. I decided to be a Buddhist monk.

Unfortunately, I had another episode with my mind. On 11/11/2004, I began to hear voices again. The voices told me to drive around the twin cities making a figure 8. I remember, I asked the question, "Why? Why? Who are you? What do you want from me? You did this to me once in 1997." Then I heard a clear and strong voice, "Just do it, my son. You'll know."

I started on north 694 freeway, turned south on 35w, turned west to 494, turned south on 35w and then turned east to 494. I made a figure 8 around the St Paul and Minneapolis city. It took me about two hours to complete the trip. After I completed the trip, I said, "Father, it's finished." I didn't feel any different after I completed the trip. Then I heard the voice again, "Again, my son." I said, "Father, do you want me to do that again? What for, Father?" A clear and loud voice came to me, "Why don't you measure it?" I thought to myself, "Measure what?" Then it dawned on me. Ha, I'm going to measure the distance at each point. I came up with interesting numbers. As I put the figure "8" on its side as a symbol for infinity, one side is "666" and the other side is "777". It dawned on to me that God loves man infinitely.

Many things happened during the month of November 2004. I heard so many voices that I thought to myself, "I'm really losing my mind. God help me. God, I really need your help right now." After I asked God for help, a clear and strong voice came to me. The voice said, "Drive east." I ask, "Why east?" The voice said, "Just go east my son." So I drove deep into Wisconsin. Then I heard a clear and strong voice again, "Now turn back." I proceeded to turn back to Minnesota. On my way back to Minnesota, I noticed many semi-trucks lining up on the freeway. One semi-truck cut in front of me. I tried to pass it. Then I heard the voice again. It seemed to come from the driver. It said, "Please flash your headlight at me." So I turned on my high beam several times. Then the voice came to me again, "Thank you, Lord. Bless me." I said, "May God bless you." And I moved on.

The 6th semi-truck asked me to do the same thing. I finally asked the 6th semi-truck, "Why do all of you call me Lord?" The voice came back to me was, "You are not just a human." I asked, "Who are you?" The voice said, "I'm the wanderer." So I proceeded to go home. As I was about to exit the freeway at 60 miles per hour, a 7th semi-truck cut in front of me again. Then I heard the voice again, "Please let me take you home." I pressed on the brake. My car dropped in speed from 60 to 40 mph. As I drove behind the 7th semi-truck, I heard the voice coming from the driver. The voice said, "From now on, we'll take care of you. Please learn to filter the voices." I followed the 7th semi-truck all the way to my home. The 7th semi-truck stopped near my home, I just stopped my car behind him for about five minutes. I thought to myself, "Is this real? Is this truck really stopping in front of me?" Then I heard the voice again, "Please go home and rest."

I heard a lot of voices for several days. I heard so many voices that I had a headache. One night, as I laid there on my sofa, rubbing the right side of my head, my cat, Leo, came along and started to lick the right side of my head until my headache went away. I told this to a close friend and my wife, but they didn't believe me. From that day on, I really loved and cared for my cat. He is a beautiful cat. He looks like a tiger or even like a lion. I adopted him from a Buddhist temple. When we met each other at the temple, we knew we were made for each other. He loved me, and I loved him.

When my wife came back from Cambodia in late November, I told her about my figure 8 trip around the twin cities and about my encountered with the seven semi-trucks who called themselves the wanderers. She was concerned and wanted me to see a doctor. I said, "I'm OK!" But she insisted that I go to see a doctor.

We went to see the doctor in December; I explained to my doctor that I heard voices. The voices told me to drive around the twin cities, making a figure 8. I also told him about my encounter with seven semi-trucks who called themselves the "Wanderers." My doctor said that I'm under psychosis state and needed to be hospitalized. I said, "I'm fine. Don't you see God is trying to tell us something? I'm not going to the hospital." I walked out of the doctor office. My wife was still consulting with the doctor. He told my wife, "Please bring him to the hospital. He needs help."

My wife dropped me at my trailer home. I was nervous. I didn't want to go to the hospital. I didn't stay home for the rest of the day due to the fear of being committed into a hospital. That night I saw a squad car pass by my home without the headlights on as I was waiting at the parking lot to see what happened. I said, "This is set. I'm going out of town." I called my sister and told her what had happen. She said, "Please come to my home, and we'll figure what to do."

I went to my sister's house in Rochester, Minnesota. Once I got there we discussed what had happened, and I explained to her about my figure 8 trip around the twin cities and my encounter with the wanderers. I told her the figure 8 was a message of infinite unconditional LOVE from God, the Creator. She said, "Bong Vuth, I'm a nurse. I think, you are sick. No wanderers are going to take care of you. You are just a human. There is no God telling you all this." I was very upset when I heard that from sister. I felt so alone. I have loss all my close friends. They are afraid of me. They think that I would hurt them and their family. Even my neighbor told their children not to play with my children.

The only person who was on my side was God. I prayed to Him a lot. Then I asked my sister, Kimyear. "Can I stay with you for a while?" I could see the concern on her face, so

I said, "Maybe I should become a monk since I'm not doing anything useful anyway." My sister really liked the idea.

I was planning to become a monk at a temple in Rochester, Minnesota, but my sisters suggested that I should become a monk in Cambodia. It is Cambodian tradition to have an elder son become a monk to honor their parents. I agreed.

The only problem was to get an airline ticket so that I could come back within three weeks. My employer allowed me to be absent for only three weeks. I asked my supervisor for six months leave of absence, but it was denied due to personnel reasons. I prayed to God, "Father, if you want me to be a monk, please make everything happen for me." Within an hour, I heard the good news. They have one ticket left for me to go to Cambodia on the next day flight. I said, "Yes, thank you, Father. Now I know you want me to be a monk."

I arrived in Cambodia on December 21, 2004. I became a Buddhist monk on December

26, the day of the Asian Tsunami that killed so many people. I was shocked. I had a burning question for God, "Why is there such a tragedy on my special day as a monk? The event on December 26 really disturbed me. As a result, I said, "May God bless your soul." Then I felt peacefulness within me.

When I was a Buddhist monk for seven days, I felt so peaceful with myself. I wasn't worried about money, job or anything. A monk is not allowed to consume any meal after 12:00 pm. My fellow monks were concerned about my well-being. They told to me to eat more food for lunch, but I just ate as normal as I could. I didn't feel hungry at night at all. Actually, I felt such a warmness in my whole body.

When I came back to the states, I consulted with the elders and monks at the temple in Minnesota. I asked, "Why is there an earthquake on the day I became a monk?" The answer was, "Because you have great bun." Bun in Khmer means positive karma. I still wasn't happy with the answer. Was it just a coincident? But I don't believe in coincident. I believe everything that happens has a purpose. Then I asked again, "Why there were so many lives that were lost? Why my bun didn't help them?" The elders said, "Things happen for a reason and for the purpose that we may not understand. Please just send them your blessing for their souls." I said, "I already did." The elders said, "Well done, my grandson."

I invited one of the elders to stay with me in my trailer home. He poured holy water on me every morning before I went to work. He stayed with me for about a month.

Since 1983 when I immersed myself into the field of science and engineering, I always felt disconnected from other humans, animals and nature. That is about to change in early 2006 when I picked up a book on Quantum physics. I learned that the fundamental makeup of matter is just energy and empty space. I also learned that this quanta of energy moves at the speed of light which is at 186,000 miles per second. Quantum physics also explains the theory of non-locality. This means that one can cause an instantaneous affect on other particle or matter at the opposite side of universe.

With this simple knowledge, I realized that everything is made up of energy or light. It is just vibrating at different frequency. That is when I realized that we are ONE and the same. I believe God is made up of the same energy. He is just vibrating at different frequency. Thus, I feel I'm one with God, the Creator.

This God-realization or self-realization really made me into a new person. I felt love for myself and toward other sentient being. I wish others would feel the same way. I thought, "If others felt the way as I, then there would be peace, love and kindness in this world. There wouldn't be war. There wouldn't be any killing going on. Because we are ONE and the same." Then a thought came to me, "What happens to my consciousness when I die?" It just dawned on me that since we are made of energy or light, our consciousness or soul will never die. It just transformed. Then I remembered the Newton's Law of conservation from physics class, which stated that there is no loss in energy, it just transforms from one form to another. Then I thought, "Does my consciousness need a body or brain to survive?" The answer came to me, "No, my consciousness or soul lives on. It never dies."

With that realization, I stopped fearing death. I began to have no fear in my life. I stopped fearing about losing my job, lack of money, bad relationship, etc. I thought, "How can I help out all sentient being from pains and suffering? How can I help humanity as a whole?" I also began to feel the connection with all things, the oneness feeling. I used to feel the disconnectedness from all things for a long time. It almost destroyed me, mentally. God has saved my soul. Now I see the love and light in all God's creation, not all the ugliness, pains and suffering that I used to see.

I'm very grateful that God sent me an angel, a beautiful blond woman who was working for Wilson Leather store. If I have one more wish before I'll pass on from this earth, I would like to meet this blond woman again. I would like to say, "Thank you. You have been blessed by God, and you have saved my soul."

I had a burning question to God. I asked, "Who am I? What is my life purpose here on earth? What is my mission?" I remember from my March 1997 accident I said to the state troopers, "God sent me on a mission." That statement never left my soul.

I was determined to get to the bottom of it. I prayed and prayed for the answer, but I never received any answers. Then I read about regression hypnosis, which claimed it could help a person go back to past events even past life. I thought, "This is maybe my answer that I've been seeking for a long time." I went on the internet and found a hypnosis therapist, Maggie who has an office in the store in Oakdale, my hometown. I Thought, "Why didn't I know about this store before? Why did it take me 9 years to discover this metaphysical store?" I called Maggie, but no one answered the phone, so I left her a message. She never called me back. I was anxious to find out what I could find out about me.

I went to her office. I met someone by the name Barbara. She told me, "Maggie is in Peru. She'll be back to work on March 15." I thought, "Hmm, March 15 is the 9th anniversary of my car accident that changed my life spiritually forever." Then I thought, "There must be a connection here. I have to have this regression hypnosis done on me."

Chapter 8: Regression Hypnosis

On March 14, 2006, I called Maggie at her home. She answered the phone. She said I could come for the first session on March 15 at 3:00 pm. She said the first session was just to get to know each other.

She had me fill out a few forms. In the mean time, I gave her all the papers that I had written so far to her. I said, "Please read the article from the local newspaper first." I said I couldn't remember saying to the state troopers, "God sent me on a mission." I just wanted to go back to that time period. It could maybe shed some light on why I'm here on earth. I told her I didn't want to go to my childhood period.

She said, "Oh, I read about this story in the paper back in 1997, so it was you." I said, "Yes, it was me." I also showed her my figure 8 trip around the twin cities. She said, "You did that. Very interesting." Then I asked, "Can you help me?" She said, "Yes, let me get connecting with God."

She touched both of my hands and closed her eyes. I was compelled to close my eyes. There was quietness in the room for a while. Then she opened her eyes and said, "There is a small dark energy around you. Your March 1997 accident was caused by this dark energy. You have a Master soul, an Ascended Master soul. You already knew what is your mission." Then she said, "You don't need a regression hypnosis. You know that would require two hours." I said, "I really want to have done on me, just to be sure." She said, "OK. Do you want to do it next week?" I said, "How about tomorrow?" She looked at her schedule and said that couldn't be done.

We got together again for the regression hypnosis on Friday March 17, 2006, at 3:00 pm. I was very nervous. I heard from other people who said that it could be dangerous, and some people just couldn't get into a hypnosis state or trance. I told her I didn't know what to expect. I also said that I may never get into a hypnosis state. She said, "Don't worry. We'll take all time necessary to get you into the right state."

I went into a hypnosis state after she completed her statements to put me into a hypnosis state. I couldn't move my body. I could feel, remember and hear things around me, but I just couldn't move. I couldn't even open my eyes.

During this session, I journeyed through three levels. The first level, I encountered a wise man who said he would lead me to the true knowledge. The second level, I encountered various colored light beings where I met my earthly father who was executed in 1975. The third level, I met the Creator, Mother and Father. I have uploaded a video called "My Journey to the Spirit Realm" on Youtube. You may want to view it. I believe you would like it.

Chapter 9: Encountered with The Uriantia Book

Since I left the Christian kingdom in 2004 to search for the truth, I have been exposed to Islam, Hindu and New Age ideologies. I was more confused than before, but one thing that I know for sure was that Jesus lives, and He saved my life. I always love Jesus.

One Friday night in September 2009, I prayed to God for guidance to enlighten my mind and soul. I placed my hands on the monitor and said the prayer. Then I typed "God truths" in Google searching engine. The Urantia Book came up.

Since September 2009, I have been intensely studying the Urantia Book. I love this book. There are many new concepts that ring true to me such as no hell, a fragment of God residing within our mind etc. The book claimed that God has over 700,000 Sons like Jesus. They called these Sons the Creator Sons.

The finite and imperfect being like us would take about 250 million years to become a perfected being who could be in the present of the Father. Earth is our nativity planet where we live our first life. After our first life on earth, there will be endless life on architectural planets.

The book also claimed that Christianity is a cocoon of the new religion which will embraced the concepts within the Urantia Book.

However, as of 2014, I am not satisfied with the Urantia Book. I had more questions than answers. Thus, my search for truths continues.

Chapter 10: Returning to the Christian Kingdom

Since 2015, I have been slowly returning to the Christian kingdom. I have made a 360 degree turn of my spiritual experience. When I left the Christian church in 2004, there were three concepts that I needed answered: a place called Hell, the original sin and salvation plan through Jesus Christ. I could not find my answers through other sources. Therefore, I am returning to the Christian kingdom. I love Jesus dearly. I never stopped loving Him even after I left the Christian church in 2004. Jesus brought God to us as a Father. I think that is a beautiful concept, and no other religion could claim that way. Also, Christians claimed that we would instantly transform into a perfected being after we die. I love this concept and I feel it is the truth. Let the journey begin again! Please pray for me and welcome me back to the kingdom…

Made in the USA
Monee, IL
18 June 2023